A Sunny Day

by Lola M. Schaefer

Consulting Editor: Gail Saunders-Smith, Ph.D.

Consultant: Chris S. Orr, Certified Consulting
Meteorologist, American Meteorological Society

Pebble Books

an imprint of Capstone Press
Mankato, Minnesota

Pebble Books are published by Capstone Press
818 North Willow Street, Mankato, Minnesota 56001
http://www.capstone-press.com

Library of Congress Cataloging-in-Publication Data
Schaefer, Lola M., 1950–
    A sunny day/by Lola M. Schaefer.
    p. cm.—(What kind of day is it?)
    Includes bibliographical references and index.
    Summary: Simple text and photographs describe some things that people see
and do on a sunny day.
    ISBN 0-7368-0406-4
    1. Solar radiation—Juvenile literature. 2. Sunshine—Juvenile literature.
[1. Sunshine.] I. Title. II. Series.
QC911.2.S3 2000
551.5′271—DC21   99-19413
                                                                              CIP

Note to Parents and Teachers

The series What Kind of Day Is It? supports national science
standards for units on basic features of the earth. The series also
shows that short-term weather conditions can change daily. This
book describes and illustrates what happens on a sunny day. The
photographs support emergent readers in understanding the text.
The repetition of words and phrases helps emergent readers learn
new words. This book also introduces emergent readers to subject-
specific vocabulary words, which are defined in the Words to Know
section. Emergent readers may need assistance to read some words
and to use the Table of Contents, Words to Know, Read More,
Internet Sites, and Index/Word List sections of the book.

Table of Contents

Sunny Day 5

Sun and Sky 7

Plants and Animals 13

People 17

Words to Know 22

Read More 23

Internet Sites 23

Index/Word List 24

Today is a sunny day.

6

The sun shines
on a sunny day.

The sky is blue
on a sunny day.

The sky has few clouds on a sunny day.

Plants grow
on a sunny day.

The sun warms animals
on a sunny day.

People see shadows
on a sunny day.

People wear sunglasses
on a sunny day.

20

Friends have a picnic
on a sunny day.

Words to Know

picnic—a meal that is eaten outside

shadow—a dark shape made when something blocks light; shadows are short when the sun is high in the sky; shadows are long when the sun is low in the sky.

sun—a star that gives Earth light and warmth; the sun is about 93 million miles (150 million kilometers) from Earth.

sunglasses—glasses that people wear to protect their eyes from bright sunlight

Read More

Kosek, Jane Kelly. *What's Inside the Sun?* The What's Inside Library. New York: PowerKids Press, 1999.

Palmer, Joy. *Sunshine.* First Starts. Austin, Texas: Raintree Steck-Vaughn, 1993.

Saunders-Smith, Gail. *Sunshine.* Weather. Mankato, Minn.: Pebble Books, 1998.

Internet Sites

Roofus' Solar Home
http://www.eren.doe.gov/roofus

Solar Learning Activities
http://solar.physics.montana.edu/YPOP/Classroom/index.html

The Sun: Man's Friend and Foe
http://hyperion.advanced.org/15215/index_2.html

You Can Do It: Build A Greenhouse
http://www.looklearnanddo.com/documents/super_salads_project.html

Index/Word List

animals, 15
blue, 9
clouds, 11
day, 5, 7, 9, 11, 13,
    15, 17, 19, 21
few, 11
friends, 21
grow, 13
people, 17, 19
picnic, 21
plants, 13

see, 17
shadows, 17
shines, 7
sky, 9, 11
sun, 7, 15
sunglasses, 19
sunny, 5, 7, 9, 11, 13,
    15, 17, 19, 21
today, 5
warms, 15
wear, 19

Word Count: 65
Early-Intervention Level: 6

Editorial Credits
Martha E. H. Rustad, editor; Abby Bradford, Bradfordesign, Inc., cover designer;
    Heidi Schoof, photo researcher

Photo Credits
Bay Hippisley/FPG International LLC, cover
Cheryl A. Ertelt, 18
Index Stock Imagery/Richard Wood (1993), 1
Photophile/Robert W. Ginn, 14; Richard Cummins, 16
Shaffer Photography/James L. Shaffer, 6
Visuals Unlimited/Jeff Greenberg, 4, 10, 20; Mark E. Gibson, 8, 12